ALL STARS
ONE TEAM · ONE SEASON

FOR MY CHILDREN, MATTHEW AND MARK. AND FOR THEIR FATHER, CHRIS.

ALL STARS

ONE TEAM · ONE SEASON

PHOTOGRAPHY BY KELLY LaDUKE

INTRODUCTION BY TIM McCARVER

LONGSTREET PRESS · UMBRA EDITIONS

Published by
LONGSTREET PRESS, INC.
A subsidiary of Cox Newspapers,
A Division of Cox Enterprises, Inc.
2140 Newmarket Parkway
Suite 118
Marietta, GA 30067

Copyright © 1996
UMBRA EDITIONS, INC.

Photographs copyright © 1996
KELLY LaDUKE

Essay copyright © 1996
TIM McCARVER

Printed in Hong Kong

1st printing 1996

Library of Congress Catalog Card
Number: 95-80232

ISBN 1-56352-272-1

Book design by Paul Carlos
Jacket design by Paul Carlos
Jacket photograph by Kelly LaDuke

AN UMBRA EDITIONS BOOK

Umbra Editions, Inc.
180 Varick Street
New York, New York 10014

ACKNOWLEDGMENTS
Thanks to Kathy Ryan of
The New York Times Magazine for
her insight and inspiration; to
Catherine Chermayeff and
Nan Richardson of Umbra Editions,
for their generous assistance;
to Black Dog Labs for all of their
efforts, and, especially, to
the 1994 Lake Lucina All-Star Team.

Umbra Editions
would like to particularly thank:
John Yow at Longstreet for his
efficiency and charm, Chris Tomascino
and Jonathan Diamond at R.L.R. for
their good-humored intercessions,
Tim McCarver for his poignant text,
Kathy McCarver Mnuchin for sage
baseball counsel, Kathy Ryan,
whose warm heart and unerring eye
drew the players in this project
together, and Gordon Goff and
Kelly Steis at Palace Press,
printers extraordinaire.

Grateful acknowledgement for
permission to reprint quotes from:
The Artful Dodger, Tommy LaSorda
with David Fisher (Avon, 1985), p. 37,
Slick, Whitey Ford with Phil Pepe
(Dell, 1987), pp. 18 and 25,
Number 1, Billy Martin and
Peter Golenbeck (Dell, 1980), p. 26,
The Baseball Card Calendar,
Ralph Houk (Taylor, 1990), p. 45.

INTRODUCTION

TIM McCARVER

EVERYONE KNOWS THAT BASEBALL TODAY HAS BECOME A SOPHISTI-CATED INDUSTRY. BUT FOR A LITTLE WHILE, IN LOOKING AT THESE IMAGES OF ONE LITTLE LEAGUE TEAM'S WINNING SEASON, YOU CAN RECAPTURE THE DREAMS OF YOUTH. THIS IS BASEBALL STILL UNTOUCHED, STILL A GAME OF UNALLOYED PLEASURE. THE PICTURES IN THIS BOOK ARE A CELEBRATION OF THE TRUE NATURE OF THE GAME OF BASEBALL. THEY HARKEN BACK TO ITS MOST FUNDAMENTAL QUALITY OF INNOCENCE, AND THEY TAKE US BACK TO OUR OWN CHILDHOOD. THESE KIDS WERE OUR EYES—ONCE UPON A TIME.

THE PICTURES DO INDEED REMIND ME OF MY OWN CHILDHOOD. I STARTED PLAYING IN MEMPHIS, TENNESSEE, WHERE MY FATHER WAS UMPIRING A TEAM WHICH FOUND

ITSELF SHORT OF PLAYERS. HE SAID TO THE MANAGER: "WELL, I'VE GOT A SON. HE'S ONLY EIGHT YEARS OLD, BUT HE'S NOT BAD." WE WERE CALLED "THE CANDY KIDS" — AFTER THE OLIVER FINNEY CANDY COMPANY, OUR SPONSOR.

I WAS ACTUALLY TAUGHT BASEBALL BY MY ONLY SISTER. THERE WERE FOUR BOYS AND A GIRL IN MY FAMILY. BACK THEN SHE HAD THE NOVEL, STRATEGIC IDEA (IN A NEIGHBORHOOD OF RIGHT-HANDED HITTERS) OF BATTING LEFT. SHE STARTED ROLLING THE BALLS TO ME AND I'D SWIPE WILDLY AT THEM — AND MISS MOST OF THEM, OF COURSE. EVENTUALLY I CONNECTED WITH MORE AND MORE — THAT'S HOW I CAME TO BE A LEFT-HANDED HITTER. I SIGNED PROFESSIONALLY WITH THE ST. LOUIS CARDINALS WHEN I WAS SEVENTEEN YEARS OLD, AND BASEBALL HAS BEEN MY LABOR OF LOVE EVER SINCE.

BASEBALL'S

RURAL ORIGINS ARE GENERALLY AGREED TO HAVE BEGUN IN 1839 WITH ALEXANDER CARTWRIGHT, THOUGH CREDIT IS GIVEN ABNER DOUBLEDAY AS WELL, FOR HIS DESIGN OF THE NOW-CLASSIC FIELD MEASURING 90 FEET BETWEEN BASES. BUT IT IS BASEBALL'S 100-YEAR-OLD URBAN SETTING THAT HAS GIVEN RISE TO ITS MOST ENDURING AND POWERFUL LEGENDS AND LORE, ITS MYTHIC CULTURE AND SEASONAL ASSOCIATIONS. THINGS HAVE CHANGED, ADMITTEDLY. THE STREETS ON WHICH WE LEARNED THE GAME HAVE BECOME TOO DANGEROUS TO PLAY ON. WHEN FAY VINCENT WAS COMMISSIONER OF BASEBALL, HE EXPRESSED HIS CONCERN AND DISMAY THAT THERE WAS ONLY ONE BASEBALL FIELD IN ALL OF HARLEM — BUT THERE WERE THOUSANDS OF BASKETBALL HOOPS. WHAT WILL THE FUTURE OF THE SPORT THEN BE?

FOR SOME PEOPLE IT MAY BE JUST A GROUP OF OVERSIZED KIDS ROAMING AROUND WITH BATS AND BALLS IN DOUBLE-KNITS. FOR OTHERS IT IS VIRTUALLY AN AMERICAN BALLET, A TRUE INDIGENOUS DANCE FORM. OR THERE IS YOGI BERRA'S EXPLANATION OF BASEBALL'S CHARM, WHEN HE SAID THAT THE LITTLE LEAGUE WAS FORMED MAINLY TO KEEP PARENTS OFF THE STREETS.

THE FRESHNESS AND NATURALNESS OF BASEBALL EMERGE FROM THESE PICTURES, IN THE GRIME AND THE DIRT OF IT, ALONG WITH A NORMAN ROCKWELL-LIKE SIMPLICITY. THIS WAS THE WAY AMERICA WAS BACK IN THE 1940S, OR 1950S. NOW THAT MAY BE SIMPLY TOO IDYLLIC FOR OUR WAY OF THINKING TODAY, BUT BACK THEN BASEBALL WAS PLAYED JUST FOR THE THRILL OF COMPETING. IF YOU WON, FINE; IF YOU LOST, WELL, THERE WERE OTHER GAMES. THESE PICTURES BRING YOU BACK TO THAT MORE INNOCENT TIME.

THEY ALSO SAY A LOT ABOUT PASSION, THE KIND OF PASSION YOU CAN SEE VIBRANT IN THOSE SMALL FACES. THAT PASSION IS NOT ONLY FOR BASEBALL BUT FOR ALL THE IMPORTANT THINGS BASEBALL STANDS FOR IN LIFE: FOR CHALLENGE AND COMMITMENT AND PERSONAL DEDICATION. THESE PICTURES ARE ABOUT SATISFYING DESIRES—AND THEREIN LIES THEIR POWER TO MOVE US. THERE IS A SWEETNESS TO THEM WITHOUT BEING CLOYING, AND THEY HAVE AN INDELIBLE WAY OF EXPRESSING THE CELEBRATION NOT ONLY OF BASEBALL, BUT OF THE FIERCENESS OF THOSE PASSIONS FOR LIFE ITSELF.

"You start chasing
a ball and your brain
immediately commands
your body to run
forward! Bend!
Scoop up the ball!
Peg it to the infield!
Then your body says,
'Who me?'"

JOE DiMAGGIO

"You gotta be a man
 to play baseball for a living.
 But you gotta have a lot of
 little boy in you."

ROY CAMPANELLA

It doesn't take much to get me up for baseball. Once the National Anthem

plays, I get chills; I even know the words to it now." **PETE ROSE**

"Kids today
are looking for idols,
but sometimes
they look too far…
they don't have to look
any farther than
their homes because
those are the people
that love you.
They are
the real heroes."

BOBBY BONILLA

"Humanity is the keystone that holds nations and men together. When that collapses, the whole structure crumbles. This is true of baseball teams as any other pursuit in life." **CONNIE MACK**

"My mother told me
never to put
my dirty fingers
in my mouth."

DON DRYSDALE

"A
great
catch
is
like
watching
girls
go
by
—
the
last
one
you
see
is
always
the
prettiest."

BOB GIBSON

"The art of life is to avoid pain."

THOMAS JEFFERSON

"Hitting the ball was easy. Running around

the bases was the hard part." **MICKEY MANTLE**

"The day I become a good loser, I'm quitting baseball… I always had a temper. I think it's nothing to be ashamed of. If you know how to use it, it can help. Temper is something the good Lord gave me and I can't just throw it out the window."

BILLY MARTIN

"All I ask is that you bust

your heinie on that field."

CASEY STENGEL

"Baseball is a game

dominated by vital ghosts;

it's a fraternity,

like no other we have,

of the active

and no longer so,

the living

and the dead."

RICHARD GILMAN

"The great American game should be an unrelenting war of nerves."

TY COBB

"About
the only
problem with
success
is that it
does not teach
you how
to deal with
failure."

TOMMY LASORDA

"The greatest thrill in the world is to end the game with a home run and watch everybody else walk off the field while you're running the bases o n a i r ."

AL ROSEN

"It ain't bragging if you **can** do it."

DIZZY DEAN

"Baseball gives every American boy a chance to excel, not just to be as good as someone else, but to be better than someone else. This is the nature of man and the name of the game." **TED WILLIAMS**

"People ask me

what I do in the winter

when there's no baseball.

I'll tell you what I do.

I stare out the window

and wait for spring."

ROGERS HORNSBY

"The majority of

American males

put themselves to sleep

by striking out

the batting order of

the New York Yankees."

JAMES THURBER